The Beauty of Irises

KATHARINA NOTARIANNI

To Chuck,
May the Beauty of the
Irises inspire you as
they have me!

Lots of Love,

Katharina

Healing Time Books
www.healingtimebooks.com

Published by

Healing Time Books
www.healingtimebooks.com

First printing
2008

Printed and bound in U.S.A.

ISBN-13: 978-0-9821052-0-7

Contents

Introduction

A Word from the Author

I became enamored with irises a few years ago when I encountered a sale by the San Diego Iris Society of iris rhizomes ready for planting one September not too long ago.

In my enthusiasm, I returned to my home with about 50 iris rhizomes. I potted them in containers and watered and cared for them diligently awaiting their blooms. Six months later, from mid-April to early June, I was greeted by new blooms each morning. Each bloom only lasts a few days, but each plant has several flowers that bloom sequentially, often as many as 8-10 irises per stalk. By mid-May, the fragrance that wafted from the garden was intoxicating. Now I look forward to each Spring when I can rush out to the garden each morning with my camera to capture the newcomers as they unfurl their petals.

Over the past few years, I have become an iris enthusiast and now am growing a few hundred different varieties of tall bearded irises. I have also become interested in other irises, including spuria and Louisiana irises.

I quickly discovered that the best source for irises, particularly for newly introduced varieties, is through my local iris society chapter. Each year the San Diego Iris Society hosts sales to raise money for the club and to introduce newcomers like me to the wonder of growing irises. Club members generously offer their experiences and have information on many topics such as growing techniques, preparing for shows and also hybridizing irises. I have also had success ordering plants from commercial iris growers who sell iris rhizomes through their websites.

In this book, I am pleased to share with you some of the irises growing in my own garden. I will also review possibilities for landscaping and growing tall bearded irises. Note that there are literally thousands of irises available to gardeners around the world, particularly of the tall bearded variety that I primarily grow.

Welcome to my garden of irises. I hope they inspire you to join in the fun of growing irises in your own garden.

Katharina Notarianni

'Cherub's Smile' and 'Palindrome'

About Irises

'Bold Expression'

Although there are many types of irises which you can grow in your garden, this book focuses on tall bearded irises, also known as *iris germanica*. The tall bearded iris group includes irises that are 27" and taller. There are also intermediate bearded irises, border bearded irises and standard bearded irises. These irises are smaller varieties, growing between 16" to 27" and thrive in the same warm and sunny conditions as the tall bearded variety. Bearded irises will grow well in a variety of environments, provided the soil in which they are planted has good drainage and the irises get sufficient sunshine.

Traditionally irises were only available in shades of blue or yellow. Now after centuries of hybridizing they abound in a rainbow of colors that include pinks, oranges, reds, deep purples and some that are nearly black. The beards, for which bearded irises are named, add a distinctive look and come in yellow, orange, white, blue, purple and many blends of color. Let us explore some of the beautiful irises in the first chapter of this book.

As you will see, tall bearded irises have three distinctive features – three **standards** which stand up from the center of the flower, three **falls** which drop down from the center of the flower, and three **beards** which serve to attract insects for the purpose of pollination. Together these provide a beautiful symmetry and elegance. Each iris also has unique features, whether petite or larger flowers, same or different colored standards and falls, smooth or ruffled petals, and small or large beards. Irises with beards and petals that curl upwards are referred to as space agers.

Each flower is an invitation to reconnect with the Earth's energy. Just enjoying the many colors is healing, and many irises have a sweet fragrance, particularly after the sun has had a chance to warm the flower. Some irises smell surprisingly like white chocolate.

Gardening is a wonderful way to balance oneself and can be as easy as tending a handful of potted plants in the home or as complex as choosing to care for many plants in your backyard. Irises grow well in containers and are also ideal for landscaping large areas, particularly since they are drought and cold tolerant. Some possibilities for incorporating irises into your landscape will be explored in the second chapter of this book.

Finally, specifics on growing and caring for irises in your garden will be covered in the third chapter of this book. This includes an overview of seasonal activities which will help you get blooms from your irises for many years to come.

To get you started on finding irises that appeal to you, check out the Resource guide at the end of the book. A list of iris societies around the world are included as well as some commercial growers who sell their irises by mail order catalogs and over the internet. Joining your local iris society is one of the easiest ways to get information on growing irises in your area. This also gives you the added bonus of access to many iris varieties already growing in society members' garden.

'Royal Crusader'

Irises

A Rainbow of Color

'Fragrant Lilac'

Iris 'Bridal Fashion'

Hybridizer	Weiler
Year Registered	1986
Bloom Season	Early to Mid Spring
Average Height	33"
Parentage	Thick and Creamy X 75-47-2: (((Pacific Panorama x Seaside) x Wedding Vow) x Bridal Wreath)

Iris 'Dalai Lama'

Hybridizer	Williamson
Year Registered	2002
Bloom Season	Early, Mid to Late Spring
Average Height	38"
Parentage	Sibling Rivalry X Winterscape
Awards	Honorable Mention 2005

Iris 'Revere'

Hybridizer	Ghio
Year Registered	2001
Bloom Season	Very Early to Mid Spring
Average Height	40"
Parentage	95-36C, Impulsive sib, X Dear Jean
Awards	Honorable Mention 2004 Award of Merit 2006

Iris 'Fortune Teller'

Hybridizer	Corlew
Year Registered	1986
Bloom Season	Mid Spring
Average Height	32"
Parentage	Roundup X Crystal Ball

13

Iris 'Queen Dorothy'

Hybridizer	Hall
Year Registered	1984
Bloom Season	Early to Mid Spring, Rebloomer
Average Height	29.5"
Parentage	Perfume Counter X Re-Treat
Awards	Honorable Mention 1987

Iris 'Aura Light'

Hybridizer	Blyth
Year Registered	1993
Bloom Season	Early to Mid Spring
Average Height	34"
Parentage	Imprimis sib X Chocolate Vanilla
Awards	Honorable Mention 1998 Award of Merit 2000

Iris 'Blue-Eyed Susan'

Hybridizer	Lauer
Year Registered	1998
Bloom Season	Mid to Late Spring
Average Height	38"
Parentage	86-20-1: (Nancy Glazier x Brandy) X Triple Whammy
Awards	Honorable Mention 2000

Iris 'Sunray Reflection'

Hybridizer   Ernst

Year Registered   1993

Bloom Season   Mid to Late Spring

Average Height   38"

Parentage   Afternoon Delight X Gaulter 81-74, inv. Glendale

Awards   Honorable Mention 1995

Iris 'Aztec King'

Hybridizer	Schreiner
Year Registered	1987
Bloom Season	Early to Mid Spring
Average Height	37"
Parentage	Tut's Gold X Temple Gold

Iris 'Barn Dance'

Hybridizer	Byers
Year Registered	1990
Bloom Season	Early to Mid Spring, Rebloomer
Average Height	35"
Parentage	Broadway X Spirit of Fiji

Iris 'Aggressively Forward'

Hybridizer	Innerst
Year Registered	1994
Bloom Season	Mid Spring
Average Height	36"
Parentage	Point Made X 2238-11: ((Osage Buff x Spinning Wheel) x Burgundy Brown)

Iris 'Well Endowed'

Hybridizer	Ghio
Year Registered	1978
Bloom Season	Early to Mid Spring
Average Height	40"
Parentage	70-54Z: ((Ponderosa x Travel On) x Peace Offering) X 71-79W: ((((Gracie Pfost x Ponderosa) x Ponderosa) x New Moon)
Awards	Honorable Mention 1981 Award of Merit 1983

Iris 'Lady Emma'

Hybridizer	Jones
Year Registered	1985
Bloom Season	Mid Spring, Rebloomer
Average Height	24"
Parentage	Twice Blessed X Autumn Orangelite

Iris 'Gold Galore'

Hybridizer   Schreiner

Year Registered   1978

Bloom Season   Mid to Late Spring

Average Height   35"

Parentage   West Coast X Warm Gold

Iris 'Fall Empire'

Hybridizer	Sutton
Year Registered	2001
Bloom Season	Mid to Late Spring; Rebloomer
Average Height	32"
Parentage	Saxon X Orange Popsicle

Iris 'Rustler'

Hybridizer	Keppel
Year Registered	1987
Bloom Season	Mid Spring
Average Height	37"
Parentage	Laredo X Dazzling Gold
Awards	Honorable Mention 1990 Award of Merit 1992

Iris 'Supreme Sultan'

Hybridizer	Schreiner
Year Registered	1987
Bloom Season	Mid to Late Spring
Average Height	40"
Parentage	Gallant Moment X Peking Summer
Awards	Honorable Mention 1990 Award of Merit 1992

37

Iris 'Iroquois Scout'

Hybridizer	Hedgecock
Year Registered	2004
Bloom Season	Mid Spring
Average Height	38"
Parentage	Dracula's Shadow X A-32-4: (83-25: (Space Dragon x Tuxedo) x Sophistication)

Iris 'Bold Expression'

Hybridizer   Ernst

Year Registered   2003

Bloom Season   Mid to Late Spring

Average Height   36"

Parentage   MF120-2-7: (Living Right x F120, sib) X JF123-1-4: (F123-1: (Afternoon Delight x Edna's Wish) x sib)

Awards   Honorable Mention 2006

41

Iris 'Heaven and Earth'

Hybridizer	Lauer
Year Registered	2004
Bloom Season	Early to Mid Spring
Average Height	30"
Parentage	Aztec Burst X Betty Dunn
Awards	Honorable Mention 2007

43

Iris 'Rave On'

Hybridizer	Schreiner
Year Registered	1990
Bloom Season	Mid to Late Spring
Average Height	36"
Parentage	M 748-C: (K 905-D, Skyfire sib, x J 571-B: (G 1212-A: ((Golden Ice x Celestial Glory) x Flaming Star) x Gold Trimmings)) X China Dragon

Iris 'Role Model'

Hybridizer	Denney / McWhirter
Year Registered	1988
Bloom Season	Early to Mid Spring
Average Height	36"
Parentage	D78-11: (Spectacular Bid x Brandy) X All That Jazz

Iris 'Broad Shoulders'

Hybridizer	Keppel
Year Registered	2000
Bloom Season	Mid Spring
Average Height	38"
Parentage	Sib to Fiery Temper
Awards	Walther Cup 2003 Award of Merit 2005

Iris 'Winesap'

Hybridizer	Byers
Year Registered	1988
Bloom Season	Early to Mid Spring, Rebloomer
Average Height	33"
Parentage	Violet Miracle X Hell's Fire

Iris 'Almaden'

Hybridizer	Maryott
Year Registered	1990
Bloom Season	Mid Spring
Average Height	36"
Parentage	F7: (Brandy x Coffee House) X H70: ((Brandy x (Caliente x Pink Angel)) x Royal Premiere)
Awards	Honorable Mention 1992

Iris 'Merlot'

Hybridizer	Schreiner
Year Registered	1999
Bloom Season	Mid to Late Spring
Average Height	37"
Parentage	Cannonball X Mulberry Punch
Awards	Honorable Mention 2001 Comune di Firenze Silver Plate for the Best Red Variety 2002 Award of Merit 2003

Iris 'Lady Friend'

Hybridizer	Ghio
Year Registered	1980
Bloom Season	Early Spring
Average Height	38"
Parentage	Indian Territory X Countryman
Awards	Honorable Mention 1983 Award of Merit 1985

Iris 'Anything Goes'

Hybridizer	Hager
Year Registered	1995
Bloom Season	Early to Mid Spring
Average Height	35"
Parentage	T5235Pk: (T4836CrSh: ((Peach Tree x (Vanity x Pink Persian)) x Silver Flow) x Falling in Love) X T5240WWPk/ Oc: (Presence x ((Catalyst x Perfect Accent) x Flaming Victory))
Awards	Honorable Mention 2000

Iris 'Cranberry Ice'

Hybridizer	Schreiner
Year Registered	1973
Bloom Season	Mid to Late Spring
Average Height	36"
Parentage	C 811-A: (Dreamtime x (Amethyst Flame x Silvertone)) X B 759-3: (Gracie Pfost x T 889-A)
Awards	Honorable Mention 1977 Award of Merit 1979

Iris 'Casual Elegance'

Hybridizer	Aitken
Year Registered	2004
Bloom Season	Mid to Late Spring, Rebloomer
Average Height	36"
Parentage	Electrique X Champagne Elegance

Iris 'Live Music'

Hybridizer	Schreiner
Year Registered	1983
Bloom Season	Mid to Late Spring
Average Height	38"
Parentage	D 447-A: (A 868-1: (R 106-5 x Emma Cook) x Orchid Brocade) X Carnaby

Iris 'Sweet Musette'

Hybridizer	Schreiner
Year Registered	1986
Bloom Season	Mid to Late Spring
Average Height	37"
Parentage	M 797-1: (I 1060-7: (Son of Star x G 1070-B) x Sandberry) X H 244-C: (D 319-1: (Rippling Waters x B 715-1) x D 302-1: (Dreamtime x A 973-1))
Awards	Honorable Mention 1988 Award of Merit 1991

Iris 'Marriage Vows'

Hybridizer	Ghio
Year Registered	1986
Bloom Season	Mid to Late Spring
Average Height	38"
Parentage	Just Married X Fortunata
Awards	Honorable Mention 1989

Iris 'Cherub's Smile'

Hybridizer	Schreiner
Year Registered	1982
Bloom Season	Mid Spring
Average Height	38"
Parentage	Pink Taffeta X D 990-C: (Bro. Charles 59-12 x Pink Horizon)

Iris 'Strange Brew'

Hybridizer	Schreiner
Year Registered	2002
Bloom Season	Mid to Late Spring
Average Height	38"
Parentage	Sib to Wild Frontier
Awards	Honorable Mention 2005

Iris 'Jurassic Park'

Hybridizer	Lauer
Year Registered	1995
Bloom Season	Early to Mid Spring
Average Height	36"
Parentage	Best Bet X 87-29: (Edith Wolford x Denney 81-5-1: ((Regents' Row sib x Winterscape) x Midnight Love Affair))
Awards	Honorable Mention 1997 Award of Merit 1999 John C. Wister Medal 2002

Iris 'Art Deco'

Hybridizer	Schreiner
Year Registered	1997
Bloom Season	Early Spring
Average Height	33"
Parentage	Momentum X 1983 #1, unknown
Awards	Honorable Mention 1999 International Iris Competition Honorable Mention 2000 Piaggio Cup for the Best Early Variety 2000 Award of Merit 2003

Iris 'Batik'

Hybridizer	Ensminger
Year Registered	1985
Bloom Season	Mid Spring
Average Height	26"
Parentage	Aegean Star X Purple Streaker
Awards	Honorable Mention 1988 Award of Merit 1990 Knowlton Medal 1992

Iris 'Fragrant Lilac'

Hybridizer	Hager
Year Registered	1984
Bloom Season	Mid to Late Spring
Average Height	40"
Parentage	T2794P1Oc: (Waltzing x Warm Laughter) X Igloo
Awards	Honorable Mention 1988

Iris 'Dime A Dance'

Hybridizer	Boro
Year Registered	1995
Bloom Season	Mid Spring
Average Height	35"
Parentage	Syncopation X Magic Man
Awards	Honorable Mention 1999

Iris 'Superstition'

Hybridizer	Schreiner
Year Registered	1977
Bloom Season	Mid Spring
Average Height	36"
Parentage	D754-1: (V435-1 x Y1560-15) X Navy Strut

Iris 'Nancy's Lace'

Hybridizer	Shepard
Year Registered	2003
Bloom Season	Mid Spring
Average Height	40"
Parentage	Epicenter X 98012-9602: (Swing and Sway x Stairway to Heaven)

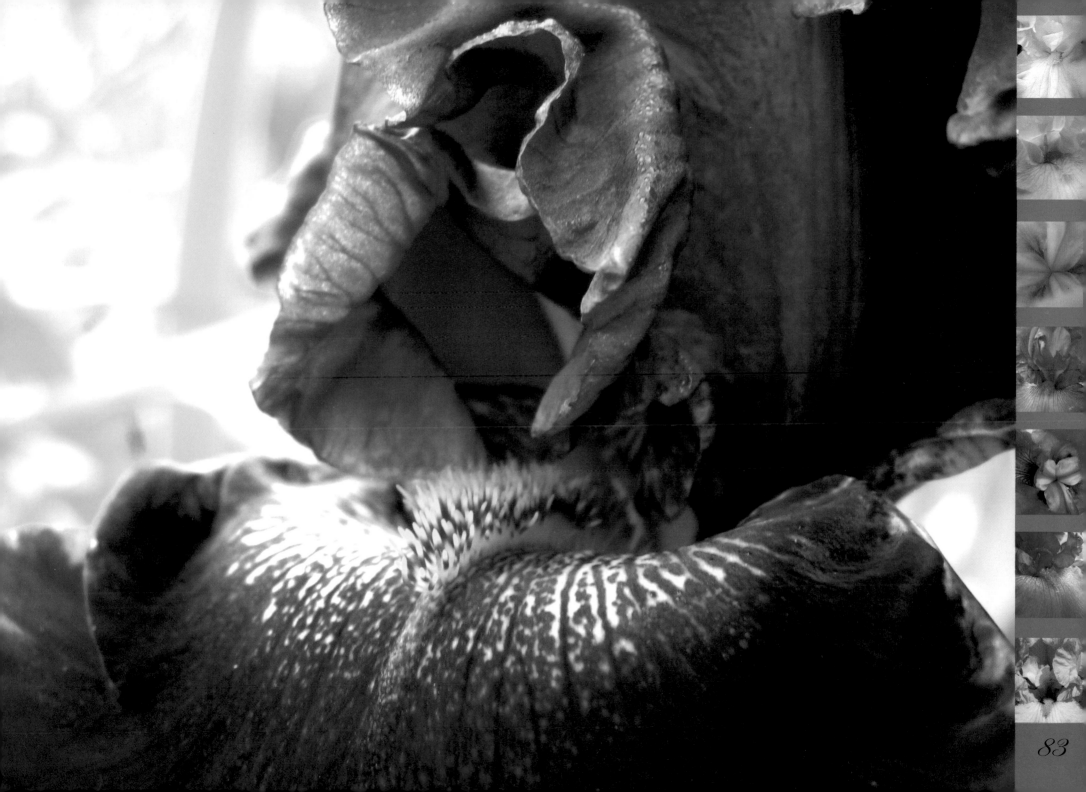

Iris 'Loyalist'

Hybridizer	Schreiner
Year Registered	1986
Bloom Season	Mid to Late Spring
Average Height	37"
Parentage	Master Touch X J 43-1: (E 575-1 x Rondo)
Awards	Honorable Mention 1988 Award of Merit 1992

85

Iris 'Spirit World'

Hybridizer	Keppel
Year Registered	1992
Bloom Season	Early to Mid Spring
Average Height	36"
Parentage	84-15A: (((((68-39F: (66-35C: ((Irma Melrose x Tea Apron) x ((Full Circle x Rococo) x Tea Apron)) x April Melody) x 68-39D) x ((Joy Ride x Roundup) x (April Melody x 68-40B: (66-35B x April Melody)))) x (Mistress x 75-98B, Peccadillo sib)) x (77-111Q, Gigolo sib, x Rosy Cloud sib)) X 84-15B, sib.
Awards	Honorable Mention 1996 Award of Merit 1998 John C. Wister Medal 2001

Iris 'Scoonchee'

Hybridizer	DeSantis
Year Registered	1996
Bloom Season	Early Spring
Average Height	42"
Parentage	1979-2A: ((Valhalla x Turbulence) x Top Executive) X B-78-651-2: (Midnight Special x Tarde)
Awards	Honorable Mention 2000

Iris 'Alien Mist'

Hybridizer	Bartlett
Year Registered	1998
Bloom Season	Mid Spring
Average Height	37"
Parentage	Howdy Do X Inca Queen
Awards	Honorable Mention 2001

Iris 'Classic Look'

Hybridizer	Schreiner
Year Registered	1992
Bloom Season	Early to Mid Spring
Average Height	36"
Parentage	Go Around X T 1800-1: (C 1080-3: ((Full Circle x Rococo) x (Arpege sib x (Rococo x Emma Cook))) x Spinning Wheel)
Awards	Honorable Mention 1994 Award of Merit 1996 John C Wister Medal 2000 runner up

Iris 'Azure Whirr'

Hybridizer	Durrance
Year Registered	1992
Bloom Season	Early Spring
Average Height	35"
Parentage	Lady X x Betty Simon

Iris 'Bella Isabella'

Hybridizer	Maryott
Year Registered	1998
Bloom Season	Mid Spring
Average Height	37"
Parentage	Sib to Temperence - (Soap Opera x Armistice) X H26LAV: ((Carved Cameo x Wings of Dreams) x Ghio 76-257X: (Entourage x Homecoming Queen))

Iris 'Baja Blue'

Hybridizer	Schreiner
Year Registered	2006
Bloom Season	Mid Spring
Average Height	36"
Parentage	Riverboat Blues X Jazz Me Blue

Iris 'Dover Beach'

Hybridizer	Nearpass
Year Registered	1970
Bloom Season	Early to Late Spring
Average Height	42"
Parentage	Ivy League X Winter Olympics
Awards	Honorable Mention 1974 Award of Merit 1979

Iris 'Palindrome'

Hybridizer   Kerr

Year Registered   2002

Bloom Season   Mid Spring

Average Height   40"

Parentage   Rainbow Etude X Jean Hoffmeister

Iris 'Royal Crusader'

Hybridizer	Schreiner
Year Registered	1985
Bloom Season	Early to Mid Spring
Average Height	35"
Parentage	I 295-1: ((Blue Chiffon sib x Music Maker) x Study in Black) X Pledge Allegiance
Awards	Honorable Mention 1988

105

Iris 'Davy Jones'

Hybridizer	Hager
Year Registered	1988
Bloom Season	Mid Spring
Average Height	34"
Parentage	T3717DkV: (Big Valley x Silent Majesty) X Titan's Glory
Awards	Honorable Mention 1992

Iris 'Dark Side'

Hybridizer	Schreiner
Year Registered	1985
Bloom Season	Mid to Late Spring
Average Height	34"
Parentage	J 969-A: ((Night Song x A 588-A) x (Y 1608 x Matinata)) X Titan's Glory
Awards	Honorable Mention 1987 Award of Merit 1991

Landscaping with Irises

'Jurassic Park'

'Gold Galore' with 'Art Deco'

Irises for Hardiness and Drought Tolerance

Bearded irises are hardy, require little maintenance and are drought tolerant. As a result, irises are being used more frequently in gardens and are well suited to a mixed border. Irises generally begin to bloom after the narcissus and daffodils of early spring and precede the roses that will bloom throughout the summer months.

You can intersperse irises between other types of plants, or plant them in waves for a dramatic effect. It is best to plant irises with other plants that have similar low water requirements, so that they are not over-watered. Too much water can cause the rhizomes to rot.

In the photo to the left, contrasting colors, such as yellow and purple, provide a bold effect.

In comparison, note how varied shades of blue create a peaceful feeling in the photo to the right.

While the flowers add bursts of color, the sword-like leaves of irises add bold lines and texture to any landscape. The leaves are generally one to two feet tall, thereby creating a green understory for the three to four foot tall flowers.

The flowers of bearded irises, with some growing as tall as to 40" in height, float serenely above surrounding shorter plants.

A healthy iris will have several buds at varying stages of growth during the flowering period. The buds open sequentially with each bloom flowering for two to three days. After several days, as the

'Royal Crusader'

bloom fades, in many cases the spent flower will dry and become easy to remove from the plant. If the flower was successfully pollinated, a seed pod will begin to develop and can be left on the plant to develop seeds for planting.

Pollination and Hybridizing

There are many possible traits that can be exhibited in a seedling, and hybridizing marries distinguishing traits from two different irises to create a new variety. You, too, can actively pollinate iris flowers in your garden by taking pollen from one plant and dabbing it on the reproductive organs of another plant. At the time of pollination, be sure to label the mother plant (the plant with the flower which is going to be pollinated) along with the name of the iris which provided the pollen. This practice will be helpful when it is time to register a new cultivar.

It is important to provide nutrients that feed the rhizome during the growing phase, after the frost but prior to blooms setting in early spring. Fertilize again following the summer dormant period in early fall. When possible, use organic fertilizers to help promote soil health. It is important to avoid fertilizers that are high in nitrogen as this will encourage leaf growth at the expense of flowers.

Quality Nutrients are Key to Healthy Blooms

Bearded irises perform best when they receive a balance of nutrients. Applying a light dose of organic fertilizer, such as 5-10-5 (five parts nitrogen to ten parts phosphorus to five parts potassium) can give the plant more strength to flower. You can also mix your own fertilizer using organic products such as bone meal, blood meal,

'Fall Empire'

'Anything Goes' (foreground) with
'Dover Beach' (back left)

and potassium phosphate. Additional nutrients and trace minerals can be derived from alfalfa meal, fish meal and kelp meal.

Working compost into the soil around the plant makes the soil more alive, supports beneficial organisms in the soil and optimizes the effectiveness of the fertilizers. Compost has the added benefit of providing humus, building soil structure and bringing the soil's pH into balance. A pH value of less than 7 is acidic, and values greater than 7 are alkaline. Irises appreciate soil with neutral to alkaline pH.

Bearded irises bloom continuously from mid-April to mid-June. Clustering several irises together will create a delightful explosion of color in the Spring. Some irises also bloom again later in the Summer or in early Fall. These are referred to as reblooming irises.

It is important for irises to have sufficient water during their growth periods, particularly in drier climates. Installing a drip irrigation system can assure the plants get the water they need. Most importantly, bearded irises require soil with good drainage. A symptom of overwatering is rhizome rot, noticed first by leaves that pull too easily away from the plant while still green and also by a foul odor from a too soft rhizome. Check irises frequently to assure the plants are not being overwatered. The top inch of soil should have a chance to dry out prior to the next watering cycle. If more of the soil dries out, this generally would not harm the plant. Later in the season as some of the leaves die back, carefully clean away the dried leaves being careful so as not to disturb new growth. The dried leaves will pull easily away from the base of the plant. This practice helps sunshine and fresh air get to the rhizomes as the irises prepare for the next bloom cycle.

Irises Bring a Rainbow of Color to Your Landscape

Notice how the soft pink and red stripes of 'Anything Goes' are brought out by the light lavender blue of 'Dover Beach' in the background (see photo to the left). Bearded irises also come in a wide range of warm colors from creamy white to dark brown. In the photos below, 'Fall Empire' makes a nice companion to 'Rustler', bringing out the warm hues in each.

'Fall Empire'

'Rustler'

'Palindrome' (left) with 'Batik' (right)

Bearded irises are remarkable for the range of blues available. Planting several different blue irises together emphasizes the unique features of each iris. Notice how the white signal of 'Palindrome' emphasizes the broken white stripes of 'Batik' (see photo on opposite page).

Companion Planting

Planting a variety of plants together that complement each other, known as companion planting, not only looks good but also keeps your garden healthy. Different plants draw different nutrients from the soil and attract a broader range of insects to help pollinate the flowers. The insects in turn attract more wildlife, such as birds, frogs and lizards.

Irises grow well in any drought tolerant planting. Good companions for tall bearded irises are lily of the nile (agapanthus), butterfly bush (buddleia), rosemary (rosmarinus), thyme (thymus), lavender (lavendula), olives (olea) and any sage (salvia) plants.

Experiment in your own garden by planting irises among other plants, or even just placing pots of irises, here and there among other plants, observing the plants as they grow and bloom, moving them around until the right balance has been struck. Finding interesting combinations is part of the fun of gardening. Some of my favorites are sweet alyssum (lobularia maritima), columbine (aquilegia), and african daisies (osteospermum). Just remember to design a watering schedule for your irises that allows the soil to dry out a bit before watering again, otherwise the irises can be susceptible to rhizome rot.

Tips for starting to grow irises in your own garden are discussed in the next chapter.

'Winesap'

Growing Irises

Purchasing Irises

The first step to growing your own tall bearded irises is to obtain rhizomes ready for planting.

Once a year, usually during the same time that other bulbs are offered, home improvement stores may carry dormant iris rhizomes. Often these come in a package of three irises of the same kind at a reasonable cost. Additionally your local specialty garden centers may offer rhizomes in late summer, the perfect time for dividing irises. They may also offer established plants in containers at a premium.

The local Iris Society chapters hold sales of iris rhizomes and your purchase benefits the local chapter. You can locate an Iris Society local chapter through the internet. In the United States, the American Iris Society (AIS) - www.irises.com - has a listing of local chapters on their website, and other iris societies around the world may do the same. In addition, if you want more information about growing irises, you have made instant friends in your own neighborhood. Many of these new friends will have irises they want to share as their plants multiply.

Iris rhizomes with clipped leaves and roots

Another easy way to obtain iris rhizomes is to purchase them directly from the commercial growers via the internet. There are now several iris growers who have websites where you can buy directly from them, and best of all the plants are delivered within days of digging to your door. The growers may take orders as early as February or March and usually will ship iris rhizomes to you in early to mid August. The appendix lists several commercial growers.

Tools & Preparation

As with any gardening activity, you will want to prepare your materials prior to your plants arriving. Have on hand the following essential gardening tools:

- a pair of gardening gloves
- pruning shears
- a bag of gardening soil
- compost
- planting containers (if plants are not going directly into the ground)
- watering can or garden hose
- labels, labeler or permanent marker

The plants will come with a label. However, if you have ordered a variety of irises, labeling the plants as they go into the ground will make it easier to identify plants when they bloom.

If you are planting your irises in containers, labeling the pots with printed labels from a label maker or marking them with a white or silver permanent marker is an effective way to keep track of your irises. With so many varieties to choose from, it is fun to order many different types.

Planting Irises

Life as a tall bearded iris begins as a rhizome. If you just received or purchased iris rhizomes, for best results unpack your new plants as soon as they arrive, and inspect them to verify you received the variety you ordered. Often the growers will generously include a few bonus irises with your order.

Be prepared to plant the rhizomes within a few days of receiving them. I often soak the rhizomes in clean water for a few hours to rehydrate the plants before planting into the soil.

Each rhizome will have a few leaves emerging from an active growth center. The leaves should be at least a few inches long. The dried roots may have already been clipped back to within a half inch of the root. If not, you can cut the roots back with a pair of scissors, leaving about ½" long roots which help keep the rhizome upright. These roots will eventually die back and disappear as new live roots replace them.

Since the new roots will grow into the soil from the underside of the rhizome, it is important to lay the rhizome on the soil with the fan of leaves pointing upwards. Cover the rhizome with soil to the base of the leaves, preferably leaving the top side of the rhizome exposed to the sun. Labeling the plant or container at this stage will help you keep track of your new irises.

Water the plant and soil well, allowing excess water to drain into the surrounding soil. Water regularly, allowing the top inch of soil to become dry before watering again. At this stage, it is best to allow the plant to start growing without any additional

Newly planted iris rhizomes

fertilizers. The plants will grow roots and new leaves during late Summer through Autumn. If it is a reblooming iris variety, you may be lucky to see some blooms during the first year. However, it is more likely that you will see your first blooms in the following Spring, so please be patient and remember not to overwater your new plants.

Maintaining Your Irises Through the Seasons

In Winter, bearded irises will go dormant. If you live in a mild climate area, no winter protection will be needed and the plants will keep their leaves but will not show signs of active growth. During this time, the plants require little to no watering other than rains that occur naturally. However, if you live in an area that experiences freezing winters, it is best to protect the rhizomes with a cover of mulch or straw until after the last frost, when the mulch can be removed and rhizomes can be exposed to the sun once more.

In Spring, the irises will begin to grow again. At this stage, they need sunshine and water to grow into healthy flowering plants. Check the soil to make sure it is draining well and allow the first inch of soil to dry out before watering again. Irises are extremely hardy plants provided they are not overwatered. In fact, the soil can dry out completely prior to watering again and the irises will still thrive.

It is best to wait until new growth appears before fertilizing your new irises. Provide the plants with some fertilizer or compost, taking care not to sprinkle the fertilizer on the rhizome. The ideal fertilizer is well composted organic material and a fertilizer similar to bulb food, which is low in nitrogen and high in phosphorus (5-10-5).

'Bold Expression'

The phosphorus feeds the rhizome and helps the plant develop a healthy root system. Too much nitrogen will grow leaves at the expense of flowers. Continue to water the plants regularly, assuring the soil drains well and also dries slightly between watering. The blades of leaves will grow nicely for a few months before the first flowers shoot up.

The first flowers may appear as early as mid-April in the Northern Hemisphere and will continue to bloom through early to mid-June. Some irises will require more time to get established and may not bloom until the second year. Do not be concerned and treat these plants as you do those which bloomed in the first year.

In Summer, after the flowers have finished blooming, you can leave the stems in place to die back naturally and cut them back when they are dried. Remove any dried leaves throughout the season to mitigate disease and root rot, being careful not to disturb the new growth that appears in late summer or early autumn. Add compost or fertilizer to established irises in early autumn to help the plants prepare for next year's blooms.

Some varieties of bearded irises are remontant, or reblooming. Although not guaranteed, depending on nutrients available to the iris, reblooming irises bloom a second time in Summer or Autumn. They usually require extra fertilizer in Spring after the first wave of blooms to give them the boost they need to bloom a second time.

Bearded irises will grow and multiply over time just like other bulbs. Check your plants in the Summer during their dormant time to see if the rhizomes are crowded and have outgrown the boundary of their growing area or their container. It may be time to divide them.

'Siletz Bay'

Dividing Your Irises

It usually takes an iris plant three years before the rhizomes become overcrowded if they are planted in the ground, and may need to be checked each year if planted in a container.

Since the pups grow off the central rhizome, one indication that the irises need to be divided is when the central area of the iris clump has died back and few or no flowers appear. Once a rhizome has bloomed, it will not bloom from the same single rhizome again. Instead the parent rhizome will grow new pups (divisions) each season that will bloom the next year. When the pup reaches a certain size, it will throw up a spike with several flower buds that will bloom that season. If the parent rhizome has already bloomed and does not show signs of delicate new growth, it usually means the rhizome is spent and you can discard it or add it to your compost heap.

It is best to wait to divide an existing clump of irises until after the plant has gone dormant, approximately one or two months following the bloom cycle. Using a garden fork, gently lift the iris clump from the soil. A healthy clump will have several pups (see photo), called divisions, coming from a central parent rhizome. Separate or break off each of the pups, the smaller rhizomes, from the parent, being careful not to harm the new growth. Trim the pup's leaves to around six inches and cut roots back to around half inch long. Plant the iris pups in the ground with fresh soil or repot one to three pups to a container, again use fresh soil.

Water the new plants well, allowing the water to drain through the soil, and fertilize lightly. It commonly takes two years for the repotted iris to get established and bloom for the first time.

Photo above shows an iris pup with delicate new growth, still attached to parent rhizome.

Resources

'Bridal Fashion'

Australia

Lesley & Barry Blyth
PO Box 1109
Pearcedale, Victoria 3912
Ph: +61 (03) 5978 6980 Fax +61 (03) 5978 6235
Website: www.tempotwo.com.au

Impressive Irises
PO Box 169
Charleston, SA 5244
Ph: +61 (08) 8389 4439 Fax +61 (08) 8389 4490
Website: www.impressiveirises.com.au

Yarrabee Garden and Iris
PO Box 128
One Tree Hill, SA 5114
Ph: +61 (08) 8280 7338 Fax: +61 (08) 8280 0037
Website: www.yarrabee.net

Canada

Chapman Iris
Chuck Chapman Iris
RR #1, 8790 WR124,
Guelph, Ontario N1H 6H7
Ph: +1-519-856-4424:
Website: www.chapmaniris.com

Canada *(cont.)*

Trails End Iris Gardens
3674 Indian Trail
R.R.#8 Brantford, Ontario N3T 5M1
Ph: +1-519-647-9746
Website: www.trailsendiris.com

Great Britain

Chailey Iris Garden
Foxgloves, Haywards Heath Road
North Chailey, Lewes
East Sussex BN8 4DU
Ph: +44 (01444) 471 379
Website: www.bearded-iris.co.uk

Claire Austin Hardy Plants
Edgebolton
Shawbury, Shropshire SY4 4EL
Ph: +44 (01939) 251173 Fax: +44 (01939) 251311
Website: www.claireaustin-hardyplants.co.uk

Seagate Irises
Long Sutton By-pass
Long Sutton, Lincs. PE12 9RX
Ph: +44 (01406) 365138   Fax: +44 (01406) 365447
Website: www.irises.co.uk

Note to Iris Growers:
If you are interested in having your name added to future editions of this book, please contact Healing Time Books at services@healingtimebooks.com

United States of America

Aitken's Salmon Creek Garden
Vancouver, Washington
Ph: 1-360-573-4472
Website: www.flowerfantasy.net

Cooley's Gardens
Silverton, OR
Ph: 1-503-873-5463
Website: www.cooleysgardens.com

Hank's Iris Garden
Chino, CA
Ph: 1-909-210-1329
Website: www.hanksirisgarden.com

Iris 4 U
Denver, CO
Ph: 1-303-789-IRIS (4747)
Website: www.iris4u.com

Iris Howse and Gardens
Bonita, CA
Ph: 1-619-479-3887
Website: www.irishowseandgardens.com

Napa Country Iris Garden
Napa, CA
Ph: 1-707-255-7880
Website: www.napairis.com

Nola's Iris Garden
Prevost Ranch and Gardens
San Jose, CA
Ph: 1-408-929-6307
Website: www.walking-p-bar.com

Rainbow Acres
North Highlands, CA
Ph: 1-916-331-3732
Website: http://rainbowacres2.homestead.com/iris1.html

Schreiner's Iris Gardens
Salem, OR
Ph: 1-800-525-2367 or 1-503-393-3232
Website: www.schreinersgardens.com

Stanton Iris Gardens
Escondido, CA
www.stantonirisgardens.com

Sutton's Iris Gardens
Porterville, CA
Ph: 1-888-558-5107 or 1-559-784-5107
Website: www.suttoniris.com

Woodland Iris Garden
Modesto, CA
Ph: 1-209-578-4184
Website: www.iris-garden.com

Zebra Gardens
Tremonton, Utah
Website: www.zebrairis.com

132 'Glazed Orange'

American Iris Society

Membership Secretary:
Tom Gormley
10606 Timber Ridge Street
Dubuque, IA 52001 USA
Ph: +1-563-513-0504
E-mail: aismemsec@irises.org
Website: www.irises.org

The British Iris Society

Membership Secretary:
Mrs. S. Ecklin
B.I.S. Hon. Enrolment Secretary
1 Sole Farm Close,
Great Bookham, Surrey KT23 3ED
Great Britain
Website: www.britishirissociety.org.uk

Canadian Iris Society

Membership Chairman:
Chris Hollinshead
3070 Windwood Drive
Mississauga, ON L5N 2K3 Canada
Ph: +1-905-567-8545
E-mail: cdn-iris@rogers.com
Website: www.cdn-iris.ca

Société Française des Iris et Plantes Bulbeuses

The French Iris and Bulbous Plants Society
Website: www.iris-bulbeuses.org

Gesellschaft der Staudenfreunde

Iris Division of the German Perennial Society
Website: www.gds-iris-fachgruppe.homepage.t-online.de

The Iris Society of Australia

Website: www.irises.org.au

Società Italiana dell'Iris

Italian Iris Society
Website: www.irisfirenze.it

The New Zealand Iris Society Inc.

Website: www.nziris.org.nz

Russian Iris Society

Website: ruiris.narod.ru

Tall Bearded Iris Society

P. O. Box 303
McKinney, TX 75070 USA
Website: www.tbisonline.com

Index

'Superstition'

'Frontier Marshall'

Acknowledgements

My sincere thanks go to Leon and Norma Vogel and other members of the San Diego Iris Society who welcomed me and encouraged me to get the "iris bug" and buy irises at the club's annual iris sale at Balboa Park. Their enthusiasm was infectious.

My appreciation goes to the American Iris Society (AIS), who maintain an international database (www.irisregister.com) to keep track of important registration details about each iris which is cultivated and offered for sale.

My loving thanks go to my husband, John, for all his support and expertise. He has been a true source of strength, wisdom and encouragement in all aspects of my life.

And finally, my heart-felt thanks to Tara and the Iris Deva, who co-created this book with me, for giving me the courage to make profound changes in my life.

Katharina Notarianni

'Bella Isabella'

Healing Time Books

www.healingtimebooks.com

Helping authors make the most of today's digital technologies to publish their works.

'Alien Mist'

'Johnny Come Lately'

(2007 introduction from "Iris Bob" Van Liere - 36",
very late season bloom, parentage Pipes of Pan X Woodland Rose).

'Double Trouble'

'Merlot'

 Graphics Worldwide Printing
www.graphicsworldwide.org